The Beginner's Guide to Goat Farming

How to Become a Goat Farmer

Roman Alvin

Table of Contents

Chapter One

Goat Farming

Do you want to become a goat farmer? But not sure how to handle the ins and outs of raising goats? Don't know where to start with goat farming and cheese making? I wrote this guide to shed some light on the goat breeding profession, which is too little known among the general public.

Especially since goat farming is very diverse; depending on the size of your herd, your location, the goat breed you choose and the type of farming you want to do, your daily life as a goat farmer will be very different.

Almost all goat farms are dairy farms, as goat meat is not consumed much in the territory, most of the kids are sold abroad. In this guide, we will discuss the job of a dairy goat farmer.

Presentation of the Work of a Goat Farmer

The main tasks and characteristics of the goat breeder's job

Basics of goat breeding: raising and milking goats

When you want to become a goat breeder, you are entering a multifaceted profession.

First of all, there is the purely breeding part; feeding and daily milking (only once a year).

In the case of free-range farms, there are also walks to the pastures, which can last several hours depending on the size of the herd, the distance from the pasture and the time of year.

In the case of free-range farms, it is also a walk of goats to pasture. These walks can take several hours depending on the size of the herd, the distance from the meadows or range and the time of year. While it's important to stay alert during grazing to see when the goats have finished eating or to identify any abnormal behavior, it's often a quiet time when you, as a herder, can take some time for yourself.

In addition to the basic activities of milking, grazing and daily care of the goats (hay, grain and mulching), the goat farmer must ensure the health of the herd (deworming, hoof treatment, mineral treatment, etc.), reproduction management (excitation and kidding), routine maintenance of equipment and buildings (cleaning, maintenance of the dairy, cheese factory) and, of course, all administrative and management tasks.

In addition to these daily tasks, there is an essential element; the observation position. It's about finding out what condition the goats are in, whether someone seems weaker, injured, observing their interactions with each other. Knowing your herd and understanding its development is essential in goat farming.

And then, of course, at the beginning you have to build a

herd of goats; buy a certain number for the first year and then ensure reproduction either with a goat, the most natural method, or by artificial insemination.

Cheese processing: value addition and product control

Many people setting up today are opting for on-farm processing and direct sales to re-appropriate the entire production chain and inspect the finished product. For many, it gives their work more meaning; they can see the result of their daily efforts and can exchange with consumers.

Various processing technologies are possible. Most often, this involves the sale of fresh milk, yogurts and milk cheeses.

Human qualities of a goat breeder

The qualities needed to start a goat farm are similar to other farming jobs. The main advantage of being a goat farmer is versatility; there are 100 in one job and you can be called on to manage administration, sales, cheese processing and "pure" breeding on the same day. In addition to being a breeder, which already includes expertise in animal health, nutrition and reproduction, you also need to be a farmer, manager, business owner and entrepreneur.

The daily life of a goat and the rhythm of the year in goat breeding

Time constraints, the key word in goat breeding

Above all, it is important to realize that raising animals is a mental burden and represents a specific burden. Unlike plants, animals need daily care, every day of the week. This is even truer in the case of dairy farms, as milking takes place daily or even twice a day. Additionally, during intense calving seasons, you may be required to work at night or late at night.

Seasonality

The goat, like the sheep, is a seasonal animal, their reproduction is determined by the season (this reproduction is called "fight"; it takes place in early autumn for birth in February-March). Goats can be de-spiced more or less naturally (hormones, artificial light, etc.). In any case, most of the time the entire herd follows the same rhythm, which allows to focus on the most intense moments: the period of the fight, the moment of calving and then the peak of lactation, when all the goats produce a lot of milk and there is a lot of milk to process. During intense periods, production can double.

In goat breeding, the lactation period is about 9 to 10 months, after 5 months of pregnancy (because you need goats for milk).

Milk and cheese production takes place from March to October. Breeding takes place in late September with calving in March. If the goats are partially free range, it is also necessary to take into account diet transitions during the transition to grass (after the winter period, when the goats are basically fed hay and cereals).

The winter period between the dry-off (end of lactation) and the following births is a bit quieter, as there is no longer any need for milking or cheese. For some, it's an opportunity to take a little vacation and do some minor repairs/improvements.

Chapter Two

Choosing the Type of Goat Farm

Soilless or grazing farming

Goats are very sensitive to climate changes and especially humidity. This is why more and more breeders are choosing to breed it off the ground, that is, the animals never leave the building and the breeder brings them feed and other food.

However, grazing, although more technical, is really interesting, if only from an economic point of view (grass is a very cheap food and most adapted to goats because they are herbivores).

Nevertheless, attention must be paid to the hygienic risks associated with parasitism, which are very high and can damage the health of goats.

Many farmers graze 6 months of the year, taking the animals outside during the day in the summer. This mixed method requires provision of feed rations in the barn. However, some growers achieve food self-sufficiency by producing forage on the farm. Thanks to the colorful grass mixtures (rich in legumes), they can also do without cereals.

It should be noted that grazing is an obligation of environmental regulations. Green feeding permitted in organic farming is not considered grazing.

100% free-range livestock

Some farms choose to raise their animals 100% outdoors.

Completely free-range breeding makes it possible to significantly limit his investment in the building.

Two other positive points of 100% free-range are the saving of working time (no cleaning of buildings, no morning delivery of hay and the possibility of monotraite) and the saving of buying hay.

However, being outdoors makes the herd much more dependent on what grows on the property and weather conditions. In addition, the goats need a guide to graze outside the fenced area.

Agro-pastoralism

If agroforestry is something very positive, managing trees with goats is always a bit complicated because goats are very greedy and great acrobats, so you can't let them graze under any orchard or you'll lose apples.

On the other hand, goats can be extremely efficient in overgrown areas that need to be cleared. It can also be interesting to create routes in forest areas (the trees are taller).

Long lactation

In goats, it is also possible to extend the lactation period. Long lactation is defined as 450 days of lactation in a goat. Initially, it was mainly used after reproductive disorders or to bring goats in their first lactation into line with the cycle of older goats.

Long lactation makes it possible to manage low fertility without culling the goats; it also makes it possible to better manage de-seasoning in goats at the end of their career. It also gives prime goats (goats giving birth for the first time) more time to complete growth.

It also allows for a more regular distribution of production and no drying up, and therefore a smoother cash flow. Finally, the price of milk is better because more milk is produced in winter than in a seasonal system. Be careful, not all goats are capable of long lactation: reserve it for high milk producers.

One-time milking

Mono-milking consists of performing only one milking per day instead of two.

It's a real choice for work comfort. Having time. On the farm, there's a real desire to have decent hours and not work yourself to death.

Monotraite is especially possible on farms where animals graze, it allows them to spend more energy grazing and feel less need for two milking a day. This minimizes the workload for goat farmers.

Different Breeds of Goats Possible

Most of the goats used by goat breeders are so-called productive breeds, i.e. Alpine or Saanen goats, which make up more than 90% of the French herd. However, more and more founding farms are choosing to use rustic breeds, less productive but often more adapted to the soil and more resistant to outdoor life.

For a long time, Alpine and Saanen goats were the only ones used in goat herds, so that other hardy breeds almost disappeared.

Selection of Local Breed and the Open Air

The selection of local breeds, if primarily aimed at preserving and rehabilitating our living heritage, also has a philosophical, anti-capitalist and declining scope for me.

In order to make a living from these less productive and often slower-growing breeds, the goat workshop must be oriented a little differently than with classic models. Food autonomy and the quality of the finished products will be prioritized over the volume of production: the product is there to tell the story of the country. The desire to have local breeds often naturally goes hand in hand with a peasant and broader idea of agriculture and thus with free range farming.

From an economic point of view, it is necessary to minimize costs as much as possible so that the margin is interesting and allows for proper income. However, feed is one of the main costs in conventional farming. In a 100% free-range system, the goats feed themselves what is available in the pasture (in short, free feed); this of course requires access to land or abandoned agricultural areas to provide sufficient grazing space.

It follows from the choice of a free-range that we will work more on the adaptation and resistance of the animals. Therefore, animals that can adapt to changing weather and seasons and balance their energy investment between milk production and immunity are preferred. In general, the hardy breeds of the territory naturally meet these criteria.

Outdoors brings additional benefits in terms of working hours and the reduction of on-call tasks; dung cleaning and building maintenance will be reduced. And instead of spending your own energy (or fossil fuels if you have a tractor) to bring feed to the animals, you take the animals out to the paddock to feed themselves. More time is spent in the pasture accompanying the goats and maintaining the fences, but the time saved remains important. And this gain in life comfort is not negligible in work, which is often very time-consuming. And finally, the fact that we accompany the goats to pasture every day changes our relationship with the herd.

Organic Label Requirements

If you opt for the AB-labeled setup, there are some incomplete items regarding the environmental specifications.

As far as reproductive management is concerned, artificial insemination is allowed. On the other hand, heat synchronization with hormones is prohibited.

In order to strengthen the autonomy of organic farms, the regulations require that at least 60% of the annual feed ration be made up of feed produced on the farm, although it is also possible to cooperate with organic farmers in the region. Bulk feed, fresh, dried or silage, must represent at least 60% of the daily ration in dry matter (DM).

The kids must be suckled on natural milk, preferably the mother's, for at least 45 days.

From the point of view of the herd's state of health, the use of homeopathic, phytotherapeutic preparations and preparations based on trace elements should be preferred. Allopathic treatments, i.e. medicines, can only be used for medicinal purposes and not systematically and are limited to three per year, only one for animals that have been on the farm for less than one year. Vaccines and mandatory eradication plans do not count towards allopathic treatment. Similarly, deworming treatment does not count as an allopathic treatment if it is justified.

In organic farming, a spreading book is mandatory for the management of waste water from your goat farm. The load in fertilizer elements is limited to 170 kg of nitrogen per hectare. Organic manure must be spread on organic land.

Chapter Three

Settling Down as a Goat Breeder

After you have been introduced and trained in goat farming, the next step is to think about and prepare for your installation. In order to start a goat farm, several aspects need to be analyzed; budget, area and regulations.

Budget for Establishment in Goat Farming

Budget estimate of installation and production tools for goat farmers

The herd is not the most important cost item, but it is

necessary for production. Depending on the farmer's strategies, it is possible to buy goats in different stages and ages. For example, goats that are already in production can be purchased for around €200 as part of a goat farm takeover, and kids ready to calve (€300 for a whole calf). Goats can also be purchased when they are weaned (€170/goat), but they will need to be raised and bred before they can produce milk. For goats, it is necessary to calculate between 150 and 250 € per goat and it is necessary to have a goat for 25 goats.

When selecting animals for the herd, it is important to select goats from equivalent systems. A goat that has been indoors all its life will not be adapted to an outdoor system because it is too fragile.

As for the stable, the required area for one goat is 1.5 m2 to 2.25 m2. It is also necessary to count on 1.5 m2 / kid and 0.35 m2 / kid if they are kept for fattening for 6 to 8 weeks, without forgetting the kids, which will have to be as far away from the goats as possible. In addition, it is necessary to take into account the areas for passage, feeding, storage and also the space for the milking parlor and cheese dairy. The key equipment in the barn is the feed fence (0.4 m/goat overlooking the feed aisle). For a new building, the amount of investment is about 250 to 300 €/goat, and in the case of building a goat house it can reach up to 500 €/goat. For a building with kid goats, the investment amount is between €170 and €230/goat for taking over and between €400 and €500 for a new building. In the case of organic farming, the surfaces of the buildings are identical, but the building must allow access to the training area with an additional area of 2.5 m2/goat.

It is important to design or purchase a functional milking parlor because you spend time in it. The installation must take into account the number of goats and the milking time, a maximum of 1h30 per milking. With less than 50 goats, a simple platform with four claws may be sufficient. Under these conditions, it is possible to buy second-hand equipment for €5,000. For more than 50 goats, a double platform is needed with one claw for every 10 goats, and the claws should be connected directly to the tank with a milk pipe. The investment in a new machine with 8 stations (for milking 80 goats) with pipes directly connected to the tank can be €17,000.

Also, the cheese factory must be functional and adapted to the amount of processed milk and the number of people working in it. For a farm with 50 to 100 goats with a maximum daily production of around 300 liters (3 liters per day per goat at the peak of lactation), a cheese factory area of between 70 and 80 m2 is sufficient. The investment in a fully equipped cheese factory is

between 1,000 and 1,300
EUR/m2.

Area Planned in Goat Breeding

It is possible to set up in a very small area and choose to buy goat feed outside. However, it is important to know that in organic farming, grazing is an obligation according to the regulations. Green feeding, which consists of harvesting grass and distributing it to the goats in the building, is allowed but not considered grazing.

This system with this number of goats is still less profitable than the external purchase system.

Savings on feed purchases do not compensate for the loss of income due to the decrease in the number of animals and the decrease in productivity.

Goat farms continue to expand and specialize. However, it is possible to have a smaller herd, especially if you want to process your milk without being overwhelmed with work and if you want to work with rustic breeds, which allows you to get more value from your production.

Regulations for Goat Farmers

As with all livestock farming, there are a number of regulations that govern animal husbandry.

- Identification and traceability in goat breeding

First, you must register your animals. After this declaration, you will receive a herd number. An annual census of your herd is required.

Second, animals must be identified by an ear tag system when they leave or enter the farm. All animals born on the farm must be ear tagged no later than 6 months after birth or as soon as they leave the farm. Ear tags must still be legible, or if they are no longer legible, they must be replaced.

Finally, breeders must keep records of all their procedures and interventions (health certificates, test results, invoices...).

• Hygienic aspects of goat breeding

Regarding hygiene aspects, the breeder must keep a register of the treatments given to the animals, which must include; the name of the medicine, the date, the number of animals, the waiting time before meat or milk can be consumed. They must also keep prescriptions, health checks and annual visit reports.

The breeder must also designate a health veterinarian.

Advice on How to Become a Goat Breeder

The following points are important to get you started:

• Know that it takes time. Focus on what you want to do, train yourself, put together a project and finally get it all off the ground.

• Be well surrounded. You must know that in your private life it is a real shock. In a project like this, you get your whole family and close circle (relatives and close friends).

• Before you settle, do a thorough study of the area where you want to settle. To create your network, it is important to know the actors present in your territory, with the Chamber of Agriculture, breeding associations, cooperatives, but also other breeders.

How Much a Goat Farmer Earn

How much does a goat farmer earn?

The average income of a cheese processing goat farm is around

€25,700 per labor unit in both conventional and organic farming. However, behind this average there is a high variability of income. This variability can be related to the size of the farm, the production system, but also the level of indebtedness or the efficiency of the farmer.